GREEK AND ROMAN COINS
IN THE ATHENIAN AGORA

Fred S. Klein

AMERICAN SCHOOL OF CLASSICAL STUDIES AT ATHENS

2025

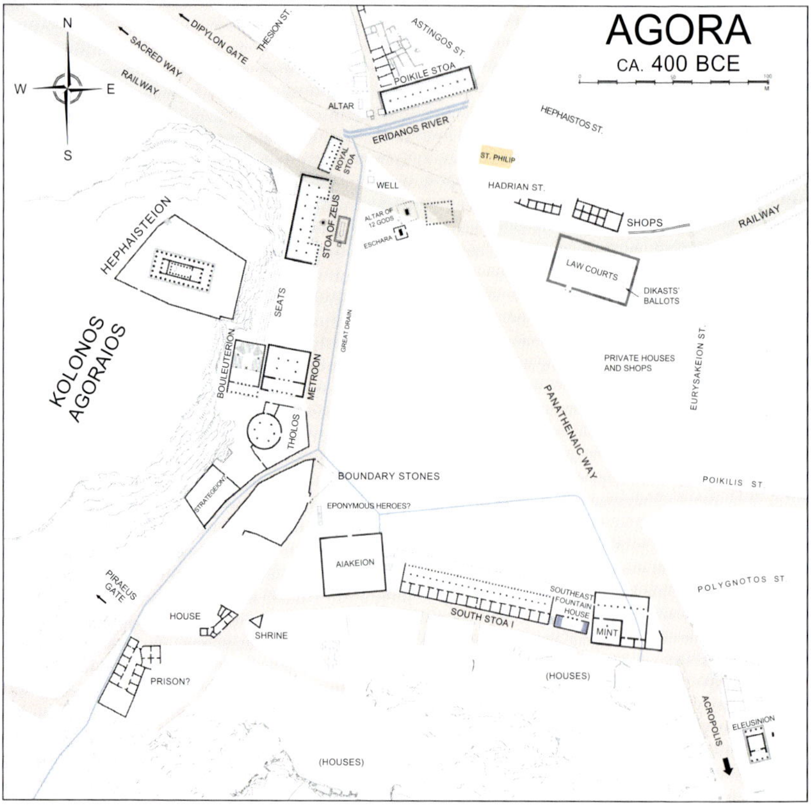

1. Plan of the Agora ca. 400 BCE

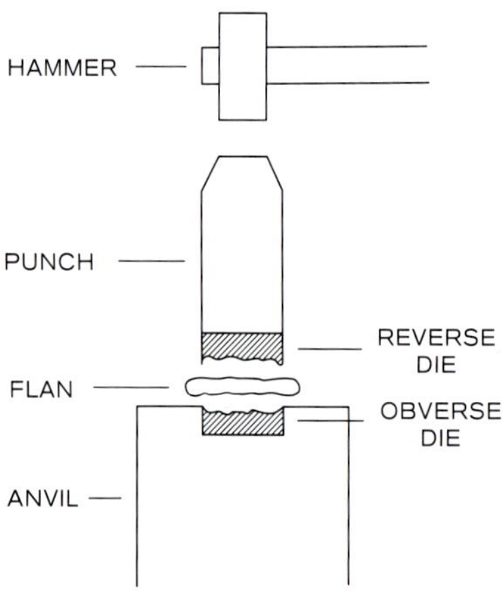

2. Ancient method of minting coins: designs were cut into two dies and hammered into a flan to produce a coin

THE ATHENIAN AGORA HAS BEEN MORE OR less continuously inhabited from prehistoric times until the present day. During the American excavations more than 75,000 coins have been found, dating from the 6th century BCE, when coins were first used in Attica, to today. These coins provide a record of the kind of money used in the Athenian marketplace throughout the ages. Much of this money is Athenian, but the far-flung commercial and political contacts of Athens brought all kinds of foreign currency into the area. Other Greek cities as well as the Romans, Byzantines, Franks, Venetians, and Turks have left their coins behind for the modern excavators to discover. Most of the coins found in the excavations were lost and never recovered—stamped into the earth floor of the Agora, or dropped, in wells, drains, or cisterns. Consequently, almost all the Agora coins are small change bronze or copper pieces. When silver or gold coins were dropped, they were searched for until found.

In addition to coins, the American excavators have had the good fortune to locate a building that very likely served as the Athenian mint from the late 5th century BCE until at least the time of the Roman emperor Augustus (27 BCE–14 CE). The building is situated at the southeast corner of the Agora, next to the Southeast Fountain House (**1**). Very little of the structure remains today because of later rebuilding in the area. Part of the building lies beneath the Church of the Holy Apostles. The mint was provided with strong poros walls, befitting a structure in which large quantities of bullion and coins must have been stored. Inside there were at least two furnaces, two cement-lined water basins, and a large drain, all of which were necessary for the production of ancient coins.

GREEK AND ROMAN MINTING TECHNIQUE

All the coins illustrated in this book were handmade. The ancient method of striking coins was quite simple and required only a few basic tools (**2**). The first step was the preparation of the flan, or metal blank, upon which the coin designs would be stamped. Flans could be produced in a number of different ways. Often the metal was heated to a molten state

3. Bronze flans and a rod from the Athenian mint

and then poured into disk-shaped molds, assuring a uniform weight for the coins. This was especially important for gold and silver coins, which were accepted in commerce because of their bullion value. An alternate method, useful for bronze coins that passed by size rather than by exact weight, is documented by finds in the Athenian mint. Bronze rods were forged by hammering and individual flans were cut from them, either by repeated chisel strokes, as was the case with the late 1st-century BCE flans illustrated (**3**), or by sawing, as was true of the Athenian bronze coins of the Late Roman period (**4**).

To stamp images on the prepared flans, it was necessary to cut dies—negative designs—either in iron or in a very hard bronze alloy containing a high proportion of tin. Coin dies were of two types (**2**). The lower die, which bore the image of the obverse face of the coin, usually a deity or ruler, was fixed in an anvil. The upper die, which produced the reverse type of the coin, was cut at the end of a punch. Few ancient dies survive today, as they were generally systematically destroyed by the mints because of their value as tools for coining money. The craftsmen who engraved such dies were often first-rate artists, and in Sicily and elsewhere coins struck from signed dies are known.

In the final stage of the minting process, the prepared flan was heated to make it malleable and placed, with the aid of tongs, on the anvil die. The punch die was then centered on the flan and stamped into it with a hammer, simultaneously producing impressions on both sides of the coin (**2**). Experiments with modern dies have shown that ancient dies might have produced 10,000 or more coins before breaking. Although only a very small percentage of the coins struck in antiquity survive today, it is still easy to find two or more coins struck from common dies. Many times, two coins struck from the same obverse die will have different reverses (**4**). This proves that the two types were contemporary or successive issues of the same mint.

4. Two Athenian bronze coins struck from the same obverse die

Sometimes the laborious process of preparing new flans for striking was avoided by the reuse of old coins, usually those of foreign mints. These coins were heated and struck just like new coin blanks. Often the old coin types were not completely obliterated by the new dies, and such coins, with two or more successive images visible, are said to be "overstruck." Overstriking occasionally served political as well as practical ends. One overstruck coin found in the Agora was issued by Boiotia with a facing Demeter head on the obverse and Poseidon on the reverse (**5**). The undertype (the reused earlier coin) is a Macedonian bronze coin with a Herakles head on the obverse and a horseman on the reverse. The Macedonian kings had controlled Boiotia and Attica for a large part of the 3rd century BCE. Macedonian garrisons were placed in Thebes and Athens, and Macedonian coins became the local currency. After the death of Antigonos Gonatas and the removal of the garrisons in 229, the Macedonian coins were restruck with civic types both in Boiotia and Athens, thereby erasing the memory of the Macedonian hegemony.

5. An "overstruck" coin. A facing Demeter head is stamped on top of a profile head of Herakles in a lion's skin. On the reverse, the forelegs of a horse are visible below Poseidon's hips. Scale 2:1

THE EARLIEST COINS

Transactions in precious metals, in the form of nuggets, rings, bars, jewelry, etc., are documented from very ancient times. Coins—metal disks of fixed weight stamped with the badge of the issuing authority—were not introduced until the second half of the 7th century BCE. The invention of coinage took place in western Asia Minor, probably in Lydia. The metal used for the earliest coins was an alloy of gold and silver, electrum, which occurs naturally in Lydia. The first coins were probably designed not for use in daily commerce but for official payments such as taxes or harbor dues. The standard unit was the electrum stater (**6**). Subdivisions of this large denomination, also struck in electrum, existed from the beginning.

6. Electrum coins of Kyzikos (above) and Athens (below)

The earliest coins were stamped with images on one side only (**6–8**). The reverses of the coins bore only the impression of the punch that forced the metal into the anvil die (**2**). Animal types dominate the first coinages of Lydia and neighboring Ionia (**6**), where electrum coins survive in large numbers. Athenian electrum coins are very rare, and only one tiny example has been found in the Agora excavations (**6**). A bull or bull's head appears on the obverse of both coins illustrated here.

The first mint to strike coins on or near the Greek mainland was that of Aigina (**7**). The earliest Aiginetan coins are of silver and can be dated to the second quarter of the 6th century BCE. They bore a design only on the obverse, in this case a sea turtle, appropriate for a maritime trading state. The reverse punch was quite irregular at first, but later, as in the example illustrated, the reverse die was engraved with a five-part incuse square. These coins, based on Ionian models, replaced the older Aiginetan currency in the form of iron cooking-spits. Some of

7. Silver stater of Aigina

these spits have been found in the Argive Heraion and are exhibited in the Athens Numismatic Museum. Two of the standard denominations of Greek coins derive from this primitive form of money—the obol, from *obelos,* a spit, and the drachma or drachm (= six obols), from *drax,* a handful (of spits).

THE SILVER COINAGE OF ATHENS

The city of Athens was singularly fortunate in possessing within its own territory a rich source of silver from the mines at Laurion, near Sounion. The Laurion mines made Athens one of the richest Greek cities and provided silver for its coins for 500 years. The first silver coins struck by Athens (**8**) differ significantly from the later Athenian issues (**9**) which were to become famous all over the ancient world. Like the early electrum pieces (**6**) and the silver coins of Aigina (**7**), the earliest Athenian silver issues have designs on the obverse only. About a dozen different types are known. Because the devices were once thought to be the heraldic emblems of leading Athenian families, the silver coins are traditionally referred to as *Wappenmünzen* (German for "heraldic coins"). The types illustrated here (**8**)—a wheel, the hindquarters of a horse, and an amphora—more likely refer to aspects of the cult of Athena, the chariot race at the Panathenaic games and the amphora that was awarded to the winners. The *Wappenmünzen* were introduced about the middle of the 6th century BCE under the tyrant Peisistratos. From the beginning, small denominations were struck for use within Attica. The wheel and horse pieces are drachms, the amphora is an obol.

8. Athenian *Wappenmünzen,* 6th century BCE

In the last quarter of the 6th century BCE, Athens ceased to strike *Wappenmünzen* and began to issue silver coins with the helmeted head of Athena on the obverse and Athena's owl on the reverse (**9** and back cover). In addition, the new coins were inscribed ΑΘΕ, an abbreviation

9. Athenian silver coinage, 5th–3rd centuries BCE

for "(money) of the Athenians." These are the famous "owls of Laurion" that Aristophanes mentions in his *Birds,* who will "move into your house, and nest in your wallets, and hatch out small change" (lines 1106–1108; trans. J. Henderson, Cambridge, Mass., 2000). The "owls," explicitly labeled as to origin, were destined for use not only in Attica but throughout the Greek world. Athenian owls soon became an internationally recognized medium of exchange. They have been found in Syria, Egypt, Italy, the Aegean islands, and Asia Minor, in fact, wherever the Athenians purchased the goods of others. Because the coins won such wide acceptance in international trade, it was to the advantage of the Athenians to maintain the new types with as little modification as possible. Despite the great changes that took place in Athenian sculpture in the 5th, 4th, and 3rd centuries BCE, the latest owls retain the archaizing types of those struck early in the 5th century.

A wide range of denominations was issued by the Athenian mint for use in local commerce (**9**). Although some very rare decadrachms (10-drachma pieces) are known, the largest normal coin was the tetradrachm, or four-drachma piece. The drachm and obol, which could easily be distinguished from the tetradrachm and from each other by size, repeated the same types. For the triobol (three obols or ½ drachm) a facing owl between olive branches was substituted. Two owls appear on the reverses of tetrobols (four obols). Other small denominations existed. Aristophanes tells us in his *Wasps* (line 791) that Athenians might bring the smallest coins to the market in their mouths and that these were sometimes swallowed by mistake!

We can form an idea of the value of these coins from the wages Athenians were paid for various types of work. In the 5th and 4th centuries BCE, mercenaries were hired at the rate of one to two drachmas per day in wartime. Skilled workers were paid one drachma daily, while unskilled workers received about half that amount, three to four obols. The government paid jurors one to three obols per day for their services. Poor Athenians unable to work were given two obols per day from the state relief fund. About 20 to 30 drachmas would be paid, according to size, for the engraving of an inscription. Teachers might earn as much as 700 drachmas per year.

COUNTERFEIT OWLS

Because of the international reputation of the owls, other mints, often in distant areas of the ancient world, struck imitations of the Athenian coins. Many of these imitations were of good silver and proper weight. However, counterfeit owls—copper, lead, or bronze cores plated with silver—were also produced. Even Athens, in a time of crisis at the end of the 5th century, had issued silver-plated tetradrachms and drachms. In the early 4th century, counterfeit foreign pieces and Athenian plated coins circulated side by side in Athens with genuine silver owls of greater intrinsic value, creating a grave problem for merchants and purchasers alike. To deal with this situation, the Athenians passed a law in 375/4 BCE (**10**) which provided for a *dokimastès* (tester) to sit near the banking tables in the Agora and in the market of Piraeus. The judgment of this

10. An Athenian decree regarding counterfeit coins, 375/4 BCE

11. Two slashed counterfeit owls from the Metroon and a plated tetradrachm

official as to the authenticity of a disputed piece was final. Any owl that was of silver and of correct weight, whether it was struck in Athens or at a foreign mint, had to be accepted in commerce. Counterfeit pieces, on the other hand, were slashed by the *dokimastès,* withdrawn from circulation, and dedicated to the Mother of the Gods. Such counterfeit owls have in fact been found near the Metroon, the sanctuary of the Mother of the Gods (**11**).

ATHENIAN NEW STYLE *STEPHANEPHOROI*

The owls, with their archaizing head of Athena, ceased to be struck in the latter part of the 3rd century BCE. They were replaced in the 2nd and 1st centuries by new silver coins, with a more "modern" image of Athena based on the famous Parthenos of Pheidias (**12**). The reverses continued

12. Athenian New Style tetradrachm and drachm, 2nd century BCE

to be stamped with Athena's owl, but the owl stands on an amphora and the whole design is enclosed in an olive wreath. These "New Style" coins, struck on broader, thinner flans, are referred to in contemporary inscriptions as *stephanephoroi* (wreath-bearers). The reverses bear the names of the citizens who were responsible for the coinage. Some of these men, like King Mithradates of Pontos, are well known. Symbols and other control marks, and even the month in which the coins were issued, were also included within the reverse wreath. The New Style *stephanephoroi,* like the Old Style owls, constituted one of the major international currencies of the Greek world and were imitated by other mints as far away as southern Arabia. The New Style silver was minted in only three denominations, tetradrachms, drachms, and hemidrachms (triobols), for by this time bronze coins had long since taken the place of tiny silver pieces in everyday commerce.

ATHENIAN BRONZE COINAGE

The use of bronze for coinage was a relatively late development. It was not until the end of the 4th century BCE that the striking of small denominations in base metal became common practice for most Greek mints. Athens did not issue bronze coins until the third quarter of the 4th century. The types of the early Athenian bronzes (**13**) are basically confined to Athena and her owl, like the contemporary silver coinage. Athena's head is rendered in an updated fashion and the goddess often wears a Corinthian rather than an Attic helmet. Nevertheless, the dependence of the first Athenian bronzes on the silver coins is clear. The owl with two bodies and a single facing head is the reverse type of the diobol or two-obol silver piece. The bronzes with two owls take over the tetrobol types. Later, new bronze types were introduced: an owl facing left, an owl in a wreath or on a prow, and an owl with spread wings standing beside an amphora.

In the 2nd century BCE, the number of bronze types was expanded considerably (**14**). Athena often appears on the obverses, but she is now one among many so honored. Zeus, Apollo, even a cicada are represented. The reverses show Zeus hurling a thunderbolt, the sacred pig of Eleusis, and the Eleusinian kernos (a sacred vessel), as well as the traditional owl or two owls.

13. Athenian bronze coinage, 4th–3rd centuries BCE

14. Athenian bronze coinage, 2nd century BCE

After the sack of Athens in 86 BCE at the hands of the Roman general Sulla, the Athenian bronze coinage was reformed (**15**). A new largest denomination, nearly twice the weight of the heaviest 2nd-century bronze coin, was issued. The types at first copied those of the New Style *stephanephoroi.* Later, the reverses were stamped with a variety of types—Zeus throwing a thunderbolt, a tripod, Athena holding a spear, a sphinx, etc. Images of Zeus and Dionysos also appear, replacing Athena's head on the obverses. Some coins, with a veiled Demeter head and crossed wheat ears and a poppy, commemorate the sanctuary at Eleusis.

15. Athenian bronze coinage, 1st century BCE

Alexander

Alexander

Lysimachos

Demetrios Poliorketes

Histiaia

Persia

16. Non-Athenian gold and silver coins

FOREIGN COINS IN ATHENS

As one of the great commercial and cultural centers of antiquity, Athens attracted visitors from all parts of the Greek world. These foreigners brought their own currencies with them, and large quantities of non-Athenian coins have been discovered in the Agora. In many cases, the foreign coins would have been exchanged for Athenian money to facilitate purchases. However, foreign gold and silver pieces must often have been accepted by Athenian merchants at their bullion value. Bronze coins would have passed by size since their precise weight was not of great significance.

One of the most important precious-metal coinages of the Hellenistic world was that of Alexander the Great, who opened mints throughout the territories he conquered (**16**). These mints struck gold staters depicting Athena and Nike and silver coins with Herakles's head and Zeus seated. A posthumous portrait of Alexander, with the ram's horns of Zeus Ammon, appears on the coins of Lysimachos, one of Alexander's successors. The coins of Demetrios Poliorketes, another of the conqueror's successors, celebrate naval victories. Nike on a prow is the obverse type and Poseidon hurling a trident is stamped on the reverse. Several silver coins of Histiaia in neighboring Euboia have been found in the Agora. Both sides of these tetrobols portray the nymph Histiaia. The discovery of a Persian gold *daric* depicting a running archer testifies to

17. Bronze coins of central Greece

the distant contacts of Athens. The Persian reverse is marked with the crude punch characteristic of early electrum coins (**6**).

Bronze coins of dozens of Greek cities also passed through the hands of Athenian bankers and merchants. As a rule, the issues of the nearby central Greek mints are encountered most frequently in the excavations and would have been the most familiar to the citizens of ancient Athens (**17**). The bronzes of Eleusis display Triptolemos, riding a serpent-drawn chariot, and a pig, references to the cult in the great Eleusinian sanctuary. Those of Megara, a town with a good harbor, portray a prow and dolphins swimming. The coins of Euboia frequently have a bull as obverse or reverse type, for Euboia means "rich in cattle." The Lokrian bronzes portray Athena and a bunch of grapes. The ox-hide shield on the coins struck by the Boiotian confederacy may be a pun on the Greek word *bous* or ox.

In the Peloponnesos (**18**), Patras minted bronze coins depicting Herakles and Athena with her owl. Apollo, the chief deity of Sikyon, and a dove appear on the coins of that city. Corinthian bronzes portray the winged horse Pegasos, which Bellerophon tamed on Acrocorinth. Aigion, the major city of Achaia, issued bronze coins with a mature bearded Zeus on the obverse and a youthful Zeus hurling a thunderbolt on the reverse.

The bronze coins of distant mints also turn up in Athens (**19**). These include the interesting large cast bronzes of Olbia with Medusa head, eagle, and dolphin, the small Athena and owl pieces of Myrina, and the large Zeus and eagle coins of the Ptolemies of Egypt. Bronze pieces struck by King Prusias of Bithynia, Gela in Sicily, Miletos in Ionia, and Carthage in Africa—all with animal types—were also used in the Agora.

18. Peloponnesian bronze coins

19. Greek bronze coins from distant mints

ROMAN ATHENS

The silver coinage of Athens stopped about 40 BCE and the bronze coins of Hellenistic Athens came to an end under Augustus (27 BCE–14 CE). The striking of silver was never resumed, but under Hadrian (117–138 CE), the Athenian mint began once again to produce bronze coins (**20**–**22**). The Roman series was halted abruptly in 267, when Athens was burned by the Heruli.

The Athenian Imperial coinage is of a special character, for Athens was not required to place the portrait or titles of the current emperor on its coins. Instead, the cults and monuments of the Greek city are commemorated. References to Athena dominate the types. Her head appears on almost all the obverses, and many reverse types represent her standing, seated, driving a chariot, etc. Other deities and heroes are also given a place on the coins. Some 2nd-century reverses depict Theseus lifting the rock at Troizen, Zeus seated on his throne, and the victorious general Themistokles on a galley (**20**). Apollo and his tripod and Hermes are portrayed on two 3rd-century issues (**22**, fourth row). The agonistic table with Athena's bust commemorates the great games, and the filleted ox-head may refer to the sacrifice at the Dipoleia festival. The Akropolis and the theater of Dionysos are also celebrated on the coins. The fractional denominations portray Theseus, Demeter and her torches, and many other types, as well as Athena and her owl (**21**).

20. Athenian bronze coins, 2nd century CE

21. Fractional bronze coins of Roman Athens

22. Bronze coins of 3rd-century Athens

GREEK IMPERIAL COINS

While Roman Athens was striking coins bearing the heads of local deities and heroes, other Greek cities were minting coins in the name of the Roman imperial family. Such "Greek Imperial" issues are recorded from more than 500 cities, and many have been unearthed by the Agora excavations. These coins range in size from small pieces comparable to the Athenian fractional denominations to oversize flans that dwarf the largest local coins. The series began under Augustus and lasted until the monetary reform of Diocletian in 294. The Greek Imperial coinage is essentially a bronze and copper coinage, although silver coins were issued by some Eastern cities. Roman mints supplied the bulk of silver and gold coins used throughout the Empire.

Greek Imperial bronzes normally carry a representation of the current emperor or empress on the obverse, together with the imperial titles in Greek, and on the reverse a local type commemorating the city's most important cults, myths, or monuments (**23**). The temple of Apollo and its cult statue appear on the reverse of a coin struck at Delphi under Faustina the Elder. A small bronze coin minted at Alexandria under Hadrian bears the caps of the Dioskouroi who were venerated there as guardians of sailors. A commemorative arch decorated with statuary was chosen as the reverse type for a bronze piece of Pagai issued at the

Delphi

Pagai

23. Greek Imperial bronze coins with Greek legends

Corinth

Corinth

Patras

Deultum

Alexandria Troas

24. Greek Imperial bronze coins with Latin legends

time of Marcus Aurelius. Under Caracalla, Pheneos struck coins depicting Zeus seated, rather than any Roman deity.

Some Roman colonies in Greece chose to use Latin legends on their coins, although the reverse types tended to remain local in character (**24**). This is the case at Corinth where a coin bearing the head of Agrippina the Younger and her Latin title has a personification of the colony on the reverse. A second Corinthian coin struck under Lucius Verus depicts the myth of Melikertes, in whose honor the Isthmian games were founded. At Patras, at the time of Caracalla, a temple housing a statue of Hermes was used as the reverse design. Sometimes the Latin legends were coupled with such overtly Roman types as the eagle and military standards, as at Deultum in Thrace under Julia Mamaea, and at Alexandria Troas under Volusian.

The most spectacular Greek Imperial issues are the so-called medallions which were struck at a number of mints. The name is a misnomer because true medallions were special presentation pieces not intended for circulation, and these bronzes served as large-denomination coins in

Pergamon

Mytilene

Philippopolis

25. Greek Imperial medallions, 2nd–3rd centuries CE

commercial transactions. Three such pieces found in the Agora, all with Greek legends, are illustrated here (**25**). The first was struck at Pergamon under Commodus and depicts Asklepios flanked by two centaurs, a reference to the god's famous Pergamene sanctuary. Caracalla is portrayed on both sides of a medallion struck at Mytilene during his reign. At Philippopolis, a portrait of Elagabalus was paired with a representation of Herakles with club and lion skin.

COINAGE OF THE ROMAN REPUBLIC AND AUGUSTUS

No Roman coins earlier than the time of Sulla have been found in the Agora excavations. Roman pieces did not circulate in Athens until after Sulla's sack of the city in 86 BCE, a date that corresponds to a tapering off of the Athenian New Style silver coinage. The standard Roman silver coin of this period was the *denarius.* Late Republican denarii were stamped with a wide variety of designs. These sometimes alluded to the achievements of the ancestors of the moneyers who issued the coins. More often, however, the types celebrated the gods of Rome and the most important personifications of Roman concepts. Thus L. Farsuleius Mensor struck denarii around 73 BCE depicting Liberty's head and the goddess Roma in a chariot (**26**).

Shortly before his death in 44 BCE, Julius Caesar broke with precedent and placed his own portrait on the coinage. His example was followed by

L. Farsuleius Mensor — Mark Antony — Mark Antony — Augustus

26. Coins of the Roman Republic and Augustus

the generals who vied for power after his assassination. One of these men was Mark Antony (**26**). His portrait and that of his wife Octavia appear on a series of bronzes struck about 37 BCE. The reverse type, a galley, was also used by Antony on denarii struck for the Eastern legions on the eve of the battle of Actium in 31 BCE. The reverse displays three military standards and the name of one of the legions.

The victor at Actium, Augustus, great-nephew and heir of Julius Caesar, founded the Roman Empire. Some of Augustus's coins stress his adoption as Caesar's son. In 17 BCE, the appearance of a comet in the Roman sky was widely believed to signify the epiphany of the deified Caesar. The event was celebrated by the striking of denarii with Caesar's portrait and a comet on one side and the head of Augustus on the other. The emperor's portrait is accompanied by the legend "Augustus, son of a god" (**26**).

THE EARLY EMPIRE

During the course of the Empire, the Roman coinage was increasingly used as a means of publicity and propaganda. Each emperor presented himself in the best possible light. The personification of abstract ideas on the coinage built up a flattering picture of the imperial house. Public works were celebrated, the distribution of money or grain was commemorated, and great victories were immortalized through the issuance of gold, silver, and bronze coins with an ever-changing series of types and legends.

Augustus had brought an era of peace to the Roman world. The reverse of a denarius of Tiberius, Augustus's successor, publicizes the new state of affairs with a representation of Peace seated (**27**). Vespasian, a general who rose to power in 69, after a new series of civil wars, took pains to advertise his peaceful role as high priest of the Roman state. His denarii display the sacrificial implements of his religious office. On Domitian's denarii, the emperor's personal protectress Minerva, the goddess of wisdom, culture, and war, is represented armed and standing on a prow. Fortune, who guides the fate of men and protects the reigning emperor, is portrayed with her rudder on the coins of Nerva.

A denarius struck in 102 depicts Victory carrying a wreath, celebrating Trajan's impressive defeat of the Dacians (**28**). The personification

Tiberius Vespasian Domitian Nerva

27. Denarii, 14–98 CE

of Providence appears on Hadrian's coinage, testifying to the wisdom of his rule. Marcus Aurelius and Lucius Verus were co-emperors for nine years before the death of the latter in 169. On denarii of Marcus and of Lucilla, the wife of Lucius, Concord is shown seated. The type celebrates the harmony between the co-emperors and between the emperors and their wives.

Trajan Hadrian Marcus Aurelius Lucilla

28. Denarii, 98–180 CE

The Imperial bronze coinage (**29**) provided Roman die-cutters with larger flans and the opportunity for more ambitious portraits. A *sestertius* (¼ denarius) of Hadrian represents the emperor crowned with laurel. The goddess Ceres on the reverse is a reminder that the emperor was the source of the people's grain. On a sestertius struck after her death, Faustina, the deified wife of Antoninus Pius, is portrayed as the

Hadrian | Faustina I | Antoninus Pius

29. Bronze coins, 117–161 CE

counterpart of Juno. An *as* (¼ sestertius or 1⁄16 denarius) of Antoninus Pius presents portraits of the emperor and his chosen successor, the young Marcus Aurelius.

THE LAST DENARII AND FIRST ANTONINIANI

After the death of Commodus in 192, the Roman world once again witnessed a struggle among rival parties for control of the state. In 193, Septimius Severus, an African-born general, was hailed emperor and founded a dynasty that ruled for four decades. The last denarii to be struck in any quantity were issued under Septimius and his successors (**30**). The Severan denarii, while having a lower silver content than the earlier denarii, carry similar messages. The legends enumerate the titles and constitutional offices of the emperor: IMP (*imperator,* head of the army), PM (*pontifex maximus,* high priest), TRP (*tribunicia potestas,* holder of the tribunician power), COS (*consul,* chief magistrate), PP (*pater patriae,* father of the country), etc. The reverse types illustrate the power and wisdom of the imperial house and the benefits brought to the

Septimius Severus Julia Domna Plautilla Elagabalus

30. Denarii, 193–222 CE

people. On a denarius of Septimius, Jupiter is shown hurling a thunderbolt, fighting on the side of the emperor. Julia Domna, his wife, is identified with Venus *genetrix,* mother of the Roman people, the feminine equivalent of PP. Plautilla, wife of Septimius's son Caracalla, is the counterpart of Venus *victrix* (victorious). The reverse of a denarius of Elagabalus depicts Abundance, the fruit of good government.

In 215, Caracalla introduced a new silver coin that was destined to replace the denarius as the standard silver piece of the Empire. The new coin, the so-called *antoninianus,* was probably a double-denarius, although its weight was only 1½ times that of the denarius. Antoniniani are easily distinguishable from denarii by their larger module and by the attributes of the emperor and empress. The former wears a radiate crown, and the bust of the empress rests on a crescent, symbols of the sun and moon, respectively, and of the eternity of the Empire. Julia Domna was the daughter of the high priest of the sun god, Elagabalus, and from this time on the oriental sun cult takes a firm hold in Rome. Solar symbolism sometimes extends to the reverses (**31**). On an antoninianus of Caracalla, Sol himself is depicted holding the globe. On Julia's own antoniniani, the Venus *genetrix* denarius type is repeated.

After the end of the Severan dynasty in 235, the Empire fell into the hands of a succession of generals. The power of these men was based solely on military strength, and they seldom remained in office more than five years. Gordian III was saluted emperor in 238 at the age of 13, after the murder of Balbinus and Pupienus, and was himself murdered in 244. His successor, Philip I, a native of Arabia, ruled five years and was followed by Trajan Decius, who was killed only two years later. The coins of these “soldier emperors” mirror the uncertain times by an increase in military types, although many of the traditional personifications are retained (**31**). Gordian is depicted in military dress holding spear and globe. Philip is shown sacrificing on one antoninianus while on another four military standards are depicted. The legend proclaims the loyalty of the army to the emperor. The old Roman female virtue of *pudicitia,* modesty, is associated with Etruscilla, wife of Trajan Decius.

Caracalla — Julia Domna — Gordian III

Philip I — Philip I — Etruscilla

31. Early antoniniani, 215–251 CE

THIRD-CENTURY SESTERTII AND ANTONINIANI

The sestertii of the 3rd century, like the large Roman bronzes of the preceding two centuries, provide a series of magnificent miniature portraits of the emperors and their families. The 3rd-century coins are especially valuable because many of the persons represented were in power for less than a year, and life-size sculptured likenesses of these men and women are often rare or unknown. Every emperor, however, made certain that coins were issued bearing his portrait and his imperial titles.

The illustrated sestertii (**32**) span the period from Severus Alexander, the last of the Severan emperors, to Trajan Decius. Later sestertii are almost unknown in the Agora. Julia Mamaea, Severus Alexander's mother, was a powerful figure during her son's reign. She is presented on the coinage as the earthly counterpart of Venus. Maximinus, whose claim to rule rested largely upon his gigantic physical stature and tremendous strength, is accompanied by Victory. The type commemorates his German campaign of 236. Concord on the reverse of a sestertius of Pupienus refers to the harmony between Pupienus and Balbinus during their short joint reign in 238. Mars, the god of war, is shown in the service of young Gordian III. Philip I was emperor in April 248 and celebrated the 1,000th anniversary of the foundation of Rome with spectacular games featuring wild animals such as the lion stamped on the reverse of one of his bronzes. Philip's wife, Otacilia Severa, commemorated their good marriage with a representation of Concord. Two female figures personifying Pannonia Superior and Pannonia Inferior are depicted on the reverse of a sestertius of Trajan Decius, a Pannonian native.

The progressive debasement of the antoninianus during the 3rd century eventually put an end to the Imperial bronze coinage. By the time of Gallienus (253–268), the weight and silver content of the antoninianus had declined to the point where antoniniani were little more than silver-washed copper pieces. The larger sestertii, which had a greater intrinsic value, were hoarded. The antoniniani, nominally higher denomination silver pieces but of little bullion value, served as small change in the Athenian marketplace. Under Valerian and Gallienus, the government suspended the striking of bronze since it was no longer profitable.

Julia Mamaea Maximinus Pupienus

Gordian III Philip I Otacilia Severa Trajan Decius

32. 3rd-century sestertii

The hoarding of large bronze coins under Gallienus is documented by an important deposit of sestertii and Athenian Imperial bronzes found in the Agora. The group of 92 coins was unearthed in a Roman house on the northeast slope of the Hill of the Nymphs burned during the

Herulian raid of 267. Only one of the pieces set aside by the owner of the house was an antoninianus. The illustrated sestertii of Maximinus, Philip, Otacilia, and Decius (**32**) are part of this hoard.

In other contexts, debased antoniniani have been found in great quantities in the Agora. A representative selection is presented here (**33**). Reverses glorifying the army and the emperor as *imperator* predominate.

Aemilian

Gallienus

Valerian

Valerian

Aurelian

Severina

Tacitus

Florian

Probus

Probus

33. Debased antoniniani, 253–282 CE

Aemilian is shown sacrificing in full military dress. Jupiter *conservator,* protector of the Empire against the barbarians, is represented on a coin of Gallienus. Two antoniniani of Valerian depict the co-emperors, Valerian and Gallienus, armed, and two Victories placing a shield on a palm tree. Sol flanked by captives and accompanied by the legend ORIENS AVG refers to the Eastern victories of Aurelian. The antoniniani of his wife, Severina, commemorate the loyalty of the legions with Concord holding two standards. Providence appears on a reverse of Tacitus. Victory crowns the emperor Florian. Probus on horseback triumphs over a barbarian on one antoninianus. On the obverse of another, Probus is depicted fully armed, while Peace is celebrated on the reverse.

34. A hoard of antoniniani from the Post-Herulian Wall. Not to scale

Antoniniani such as these have proved to be invaluable dating tools for the excavators of the Agora. A classic example is the hoard of 16 coins (**34**) found in the fabric of the Post-Herulian Wall. The antoniniani run through the reign of Probus and prove that the wall was erected after the Herulian sack to protect the Athenians against subsequent barbarian raids.

THE TETRARCHY

Diocletian was hailed emperor by his troops in 284. In 293, he reorganized the Roman state by establishing the Tetrarchy, a division of the Empire into four great districts presided over by four co-emperors. Diocletian chose Galerius as his colleague in the East. The West was governed by Maximian and Constantius Chlorus. One year later, Diocletian reformed the Roman coinage. The local Greek Imperial issues were halted and the Empire was supplied with uniform coins struck by about 15 official mints from London to Alexandria. True silver coins were once again issued and bronze coins of three denominations were struck. The largest bronze piece, the *follis,* usually bore the personification of the spirit of the Roman People on the reverse, emphasizing the unity of the Empire. A follis of Maximian struck at Aquileia in Italy is pictured here (**35**). At Carthage, the personification of Africa holding an elephant tusk was the reverse type. The intermediate-size bronzes carried obverse portraits of the four tetrarchs

Maximian — Galerius

Diocletian — Galerius — Constantius Chlorus — Maximian

35. Bronze coinage of the Tetrarchy, 293–305 CE

wearing radiate crowns, as on the antoniniani. Bronze pieces of Diocletian, Galerius, Constantius Chlorus, and Maximian, all from the imperial mint at Kyzikos, are illustrated. The uniform reverse design depicts Jupiter handing a globe surmounted by Victory to the emperor.

CONSTANTINE THE GREAT

Diocletian retired as emperor in 305 and in 306 Constantius died. It was not long before the tetrarchic system of government dissolved in the face of personal ambition. Open conflict broke out among six rivals: Galerius, Maximian, Maxentius, Licinius, Maximin Daia, and Constantine, the son of Constantius. Maximian died in 310, Galerius in 311, and Maximin Daia in 313. Maxentius was defeated in 312 at the Milvian Bridge in Rome, a victory that led to Constantine's embrace of Christianity. In 324, Constantine eliminated his last rival, Licinius, and won control of the entire Empire.

In the Agora excavations, Late Roman gold and silver coins are unknown, but thousands of bronze pieces of small change have been unearthed. Two of Constantine's folles, of lesser weight than those of the Tetrarchy, and a follis struck in honor of Helen, the emperor's mother, are illustrated (**36**). The reverses depict two soldiers flanking standards, two Victories holding a wreath, and, appropriately on Helen's coin, a female

36. Bronze coinage of Constantine, 307–337 CE

personification of the Security of the Empire. Especially interesting are the two Constantinian folles representing the old capital of Rome and Constantine's new capital in the East, Constantinople ("city of Constantine," Greek Byzantium, today Istanbul).

Constantine II | Constantius II | Constans I

37. Bronze coins of the sons of Constantine

Constantine's consolidation of power was so complete that he succeeded in doing what no emperor since the Severans a century before succeeded in doing: establishing a new dynasty that ruled the Roman world for more than a half century. Constantine's three sons (**37**) became joint regents in 337 and divided the territories of the Empire among themselves: Constantine II (337–340), the eldest; Constantius II (337–361), the longest lasting; and Constans I (337–350), the youngest. Reflecting the times, the reverses are exclusively military in character: bound captives and the emperor with army standards.

Opinion is divided as to when the ancient world came to an end and the Middle Ages began, but a strong case can be made for May 11, 330, the day Constantine dedicated his New Rome to the God of the Christians. In terms of the Roman coinage, however, there is no significant break in the images depicted on the coins until much later.

The Athenian Agora is today not a marketplace but an archaeological site. Nevertheless, coins still change hands in the Agora through the collection of admission fees and the sale of books and souvenirs in the Stoa of Attalos museum, and coins are undoubtedly still being lost on the site.

ILLUSTRATIONS

All illustrated coins come from the Agora excavations and are shown at 1:1 scale unless otherwise noted; photography is the work of Craig Mauzy. The coins can be viewed online in the ASCSA's Digital Collections at https://ascsa.net, using the inventory numbers listed below.

1. Plan by William B. Dinsmoor Jr.
2. Drawing after H. Besi
3. B 1046
4. N 7550, N 4376
5. N 16444
6. N 5417, N 78633
7. N 31036
8. N 19658, N 50349, N 38410
9. N 38425, N 24585, N 38422, N 28826, N 14838, N 17501, N38419, N 16442
10. I 7180
11. N 14481, N 15744, N 22080
12. N 20394, N 23990
13. N 47699, N 8948, N 38380, N 32200, N 32188, N 47468, N 36777, N 37680, N 67279, N 38387
14. N 32944, N 38389, N 78885, N 7381, N 45404, N 37183
15. N 38426, N 31404, N 38386, N 38383, N 36880, N 38382, N 36675, N 36813
16. N 33946, N 38413, N 38375, N 3555, N 12780, N 38439
17. N 38424, N 61982, N 24954, N 48556, N 49050
18. N 71288, N 51547, N 5289, N 7271
19. N 38374, N 37928, N 37675, N 8303, N 38376, N 46370, N 51007
20. N 47479, N 51150, N 31836, N 38381
21. N 20388, N 33230, N 28969
22. N 2681, N 36966, N 52507, N 18091, N 2651, N 2697, N 33030, N 2629, N 2686, N 67869, N 2653, N 2647
23. N 36981, N 1443, N 12711, N 62340
24. N 16335, N 16754, N 20946, N 51722, N 51724
25. N 38378, N 38379, N 38409
26. N 15784, N 65041, N 38377, N 38415
27. N 18435, N 44219, N 58282, N 51325
28. N 38408, N 44969, N 38396, N 8999
29. N 38414, N 29556, N 45592
30. N 38394, N 61886, N 62201, N 37037
31. N 38407, N 38438, N 65977, N 66842, N 62149, N 7429
32. N 51629, N 38393, N 15062, N 31946, N 38391, N 38392, N 52487
33. N 35806, N 27349, N 62533, N 46665, N 7416, N 38402, N 35601, N 44679, N 28790, N 38416
34. N 46346–N 46361
35. N 38417, N 27644, N 38403, N 44967, N 8917, N 45524
36. N 38399, N 33148, N 33173, N 46717, N 62018
37. N 3219, N 38400, N 63342

Back cover. Coin hoard, deposit F 13:4